To Jacq

with love

David

9 May '96

JUMPING FROM
KIYOMIZU

David Cobb

*with nine drawings
by Charlotte Smith*

**IRON
PRESS**

First published 1996 by IRON Press
5 Marden Terrace, Cullercoats
North Shields, Northumberland, NE30 4PD, UK
Tel/Fax: (0191) 253 1901

Typeset by David Stephenson
in Sabon 11 point

Printed by Peterson Printers
South Shields

ISBN 0 906228 56 5

Also by David Cobb
'A Leap in the Light'
'Mounting Shadows'
'Chips off the Old Great Wall'
'The Shield-Raven of Wittenham'

IRON Press books are represented by:
Password Books Ltd.
23 New Mount Street
Manchester M4 4DE
Tel: (0161) 953 4009
Fax: (0161) 953 4001

PREAMBLE

At the Kiyomizu Temple in Kyoto, Japan, known in English as the
Temple of Clear Water, people lean out slightly from a precarious
balcony and ladle water into their mouths in the hope of
procuring a long and happy life. Although they face no great
danger, the expression 'jumping from Kiyomizu' has gone into the Japanese language as a euphemism
for 'taking a risky decision'.

I drank the waters of Kiyomizu myself in 1977 and at about the
same time began to make haiku, soon realising that to write
these small poems is itself a risky business. For the poet must
keep a firm hold on life and draw up 'spots of time' (and
droplets of sensation) which are limpidly clear, distinct and

self-sufficing, yet which also seem to have come from some
mysteriously deep well of truth; so that one is fascinated not
only with the surface of each droplet, but also with what is
inside it and with its potential for linking up with other droplets.
If the poet can see like this, he will indeed have a new lease of
life and a whole new Weltanschauung.

shafts of late sunlight -
a crane-fly's tail probes
the Lakeland fell

*

boy or girl?
- in the ultrascanned womb
it plays with itself

your trickle of slime,
slug, gives me a clue
where your head will be

*

as the cord spills out
the midwife encloses it
in latex gloves

baby's first move
detached from the placenta
is to lick her lips

*

nestled
in a hoofprint
crocuses

red, red baby -
the father wipes away
the mother's blood

*

after the birth
father goes home to prepare
breakfast for one

the young mother's breast
gummed with her baby's mucus -
so like a plum

*

length of the beach
cries of a toddler
who has seen a shrimp

she counts the hours
by dandelions, knowing
only one to three

*

through spray
she scissor-jumps, and rainbows
flicker her thighs

how tall she is now
measure it by the scrape
under the swing

*

the toy ark
stocked up for forty days -
and ants march in

sun through the blinds -
the boy with model cars
steers around shadows

*

mother and son
talking together
in his sleep

soon as the beetle's
nicked off the balsam leaf -
a nettle sting

*

son of a leper -
hale, but how white the palms
handing me five-stones

behind the coal-box
a black cat licks the wind
out of its fur

*

the breeze this May –
going back time and again
for a free balloon

on the bunker, rime:
fingernail-deep my son
scratches his name

∗

bedtime
fairy stories, then
the fingermarks

first day at school -
in the garden only the wind
swinging the swing

*

under bamboo
heavy with rain a cat
dangles a half-licked paw

children panicking
out of the tiger cage
a wasp

*

Class One's play -
the sheep's eyes goggle
at the angels' news

the sermon over -
father matches the coins
to each offspring's size

*

egg-and-spoon -
only the Down's syndrome girl
cheats without blushing

before the bonfire,
after the fireworks -
full moon

*

our hateful neighbours -
their baby crying
like other babies

now a flock, now a shoal
buntings in sunlight
across the stream

*

impossible
to walk in the woods today
unless on snowdrops

the tortoiseshell
follows the winding brook
nettle by nettle

*

lane of wild roses -
her book-bag swinging
in no hurry home

Dies irae -
the vicar promises
a second slide-show

*

in the chancel, bats
skimming over sopranos'
high Cs

creepered battlements -
the vanish of a white scut
into a dry moat

*

the falling hail
across the old battlefield
cairn after cairn

a glance away
from tyrannosaurus rex
my fingernails

*

after the all-clear
not remembering the bombs
only the kiss

left turn,
about turn -
    fog closes around
    the squad at drill

*

sick chestnut leaves
drop to the corporal's cry
of 'Bayonets'

gnat hum
everywhere in the June sky
nebulae

*

the sun stretching
over the sandbags
the sentry's yawn

at the desert's edge
the very persistence
of just this one fly

*

cookhouse call -
overhead the circling
grace of kites

this village,
no special claim to fame,
but all these sparrows ...

*

green pastures -
onwards the horses, never
raising their heads

daffodil morning -
looking for something
very blue to wear

*

in the green lane
where they walk the dogs, even
the grass off its lead

a flash, and hot rain
big-spotting the pavement -
fragrant dust

*

dove, in the pear tree's
blossom, your camouflage is
falling about you ...

right across the park
her legs
remain as long

*

out in all weathers
how polished
the scarecrow's top hat

dogbarkcuckoocallcramp
the first moment
of a new day

*

dawn chorus -
scenting her pillowed hair
this tousled spring

in the hotel doors
the latecomer's
revolving frown

*

evening by the river,
red-painted toenails
sinking into silt

at the quick-serve till
checked out with each item
        her engagement ring

                *

        despite her pink hand
the change she slips to me
    chill in my groin

after mating
the damselfly resettles
on the grooved leaf

*

a kiss on each cheek -
traffic tearing past
in both directions

first morning of frost -
steaming into the sunshine
a cat's yawn

*

wretched scarecrow -
the only clout on his buttocks
a shift in the wind ...

from poolside to pool
floodlit at midnight
frogs onto frogs

*

the rainbeat softens
at the inn of paper walls
how the pleasured wives scream ...

on her love letters
an album of mint stamps
from her time at school

*

convent - on the line
a nun's black stockings
slap across my face

sleeping on his own
the quilt still wanders
her side of the bed

*

breakfast in silence -
both halves of the grapefruit
unsweetened

by the mail-flap
it has seen better times
that spider's web

*

making up,
obliterating the tiff
with her powder puff

wet election day -
poster-faces all
a pulp on sticks

*

to the forsaken pond
barley hitched by the beards
to wanderers' socks

the shortest day -
sparrows' litter
in the swallows' porch

*

pacing the streets
for the tenth time passing
that scrunched eggshell

the hoover gathers
from every room
her hairs

*

one misty morning
what she really meant to say
said   in a postscript

on the larch-lap fence
a dove sits in the wind
collar turned up

*

close-circuit TV:
watching myself going
the other way

on the wrong train
the fury of the man
with the white stick

*

rumble of barrows
dismantling the market -
cold, full moon ...

evening class -
as ever the divorcee
sculpting embraces

*

bitter the wind
huddling four pairs of doves
into an eightsome

that dark odour
trickling from the tar machine
those boyhood summers

*

' ... the fish is fresh ...'
his hand rustles the menu
past dead daffodils

barbecue -
hairs on the cook's belly
sprinkled with salt

*

less light in the spoons -
waiters take in the cushions
at the Greek cafe

giving his daughter
away - her rouge
all over his beard

*

towards sunset
the riptide rolling
an empty crabshell

goldfinch, your fiery throat!
yet the ants attend only
to your glazed eye ...

*

a bust of wet clay -
feeling one's own face
        from the inside

a whole palaver
about the route to take -
dry river bed

*

no seatbelt, but
the Greek girl gives her baby
camomile tea

in the garden shed
a screw turned tighter
winds in a web

*

ploughing in snow -
lining the dun furrows
another light fall

lizards creeping
between the foreshore rocks
the cool Levanter

*

the peasant scoops
from a hundred pools of sea
salt - a handful

the swifts have left
the silence
of the dusk

*

neighbours in Spain -
leaf-fall on the shared drive
awaits my besom

delphiniums:
a second blooming now
in autumn mist

*

mid-life crisis,
purchasing Valentines
- three at a time!

New Year's first workday -
a pig's snout rooting
into morning snow

*

frost sparkle
in the starlings' eyes
scattered oatmeal

the farmhand whistles
drilling with his tractor
winter wheat

*

breaking for lunch
the joiner padlocking
the coffin shed

lightning bolt -
the fax machine issues
a blank receipt

*

nearing evensong
masons adapt their tapping
to the organist

fifty-fifth November -
light the blue touch paper
and   retire early

*

'released' from his job
into the sparrows' garden
also to potter

mauled blackbird
with its last pulse
    squirting lime

*

a shift in the wind -
thistledown starts to blow
in from the sea

market day in May -
somewhere in the shopping bag
will and testament

*

pendulous willow
clinging to more raindrops
than it can retain

Wednesday market -
the smell of onions
in the mackerels' eyes

*

foul weather -
sparrows in the bandstand
on an upturned chair

lugworm diggers -
a few words on the salt wind
about mugs of tea

*

forged
in the marl hearse-track
horseshoes of ice

puffed out, walking
without ever reaching
the end of the gale

*

snail, you have wandered
everywhere and nowhere
left your shell

walking on my own
I observe for the first time
the lane winds uphill

*

folded into
red plumage   the kestrel's
black-edged wings

becalmed
under the weeping willow
moultings of down

*

in crevices
after the birthday breakfast
muesli pulp

for ever the flies -
after the raucous swifts
the unheard bats

*

supporting
flopping chrysanthemums
some spider threads

incontinence
afflicts him, yet he goes on
    tying up sweet peas

*

    drip
    by
    drip
the moonlight
lengthens
  in the
  icicle

days draw in
berries still to be eaten
closer to the house

*

-hustling snow,
settle, lie easy here,
against my fence ...

Michaelmas - a wasp
seems to be warming its feet
on the back of my neck

*

in the lantern
of the shut-down lighthouse
tonight the North Star

through a stone arch
an old man gripping a staff
the light behind him

*

sun dips to sea -
blown to my lips the tang
of far-off voices

October summer -
a ladybird half-alert
on each pruned leaf

*

to this pensioner
putting the clock back an hour
still seems important

mirror steamed,
breath taken away -
he brushed his teeth

*

bronchitis,
another bout - the thrush
          battering snails

sunlight
fading through stained glass
the laid-up flags

*

among peelings
due to be composted
a plastic poppy

stuck indoors -
a halo around the hand
at the letter box

*

edge of the forest
the sun's new entrance
past a fallen tree

out of the haze
the green-remembered heights
returning blue

*

from the ridge, whinnies
of a long-coated horse
an age coming down

by a moorland wall
green dye rinses
from a ewe's rump

*

rain butt bone-dry –
globe thistles like tinder
under the bees' feet

' ... known only to God ...'
the general reviews them
through binoculars

*

couple aged eighty
carrying a dozen eggs
between them

snow lingers on
in one right-angle
of the wayside cross

*

on the fixture list
the name of the groundsman
we buried last week

day of his funeral
still inviting messages
after the tone

*

in the cortege
not one mourner whose shuffles
fill his shoes

the pallbearers' joke
not within earshot of
the load on the bier

*

filling the grave
more earth
than will go back in

as she lies dying
I tell her the crocuses
are early this year

*

at the Gates of Eternity
I take her hand and say,
'It snows in Essex ...'

the will to live
and the wish to die -
her eyes beseeching me
to wet her lips

*

where they groom the dead
the bedtime story teller's
jaw in a sling

boats left to winter -
clacking of halyards
against sheetless masts

*

in the gale, scarecrow
in his baggy overalls
nearly all wind

the sea far out -
mares' hooves pound
over the seashells

*

the year ends in wind
scattering down
acorns and twigs

on windmill hill
the snow creases
over white weatherboards

*

in the dark garden
from a distance lightning on
the track of a snail

carrying the sun
on my shoulders, from one shade
to a deeper one

*

low-flying pigeons
the sun shining
under their wings

IRON Press was formed in Spring 1973, initially to publish the magazine IRON which more than two decades, and more than 1,500 writers on, survives as one of the country's most active alternative mags – a fervent purveyor of new poetry, fiction and graphics. £12.00 gets you a subscription. Try our intriguing book list too, titles which can rarely be found on the shelves of mega-stores. Fortified by a belief in good writing, as against literary competitions or marketing trivia, IRON remains defiantly a small press. Our address is at the front of this book